LIVING WITH INTENTION

A Practical Guide to Self-Discovery, Clarity, and a Meaningful Life

Richard Trillion Mantey

Dedication

To my parents—

Thank you for your love, values, and unwavering support. You taught me what it means to live with purpose and grace.

To everyone searching for more—

More meaning, more clarity, more alignment—

May this book be a gentle reminder that your life has deep value, and your purpose is already within you.

And to the quiet moments that led me here—

You showed me that the most powerful changes begin with a single, intentional choice.

Acknowledgments

Writing this book has been a journey of deep reflection, and I couldn't have done it alone.

To my parents, thank you for your endless encouragement, wise example, and the values you instilled in me. Your love and sacrifices are the roots of every page in this book.

To my editors—your thoughtful feedback, sharp eyes, and belief in this message helped shape the heart and clarity of this work. Thank you for refining the vision and making it stronger.

To my friends, mentors, and early readers—your support, insights, and encouragement kept me grounded and inspired throughout the writing process.

To every reader holding this book, thank you for showing up for yourself. Your desire to live with intention is powerful, and I'm honored to walk this journey with you.

And to the quiet moments of doubt, stillness, and self-discovery—thank you. You taught me that purpose doesn't shout; it whispers when we're finally ready to listen.

Author Biography

Richard Trillion Mantey is a personal growth author, speaker, and purpose coach who helps people break free from distraction and live with clarity, focus, and passion. With a background in mindset transformation and habit design, Richard writes for those who are ready to turn intention into action and make their life truly count.

Known for his relatable voice and deeply practical wisdom, Richard is committed to helping readers rediscover meaning in their everyday lives. Living with Intention is part of his mission to inspire others to live on purpose, not by accident.

When he's not writing, Richard enjoys teaching, mentoring, and exploring what it means to lead a life of impact, integrity, and inner peace.

Contents

Dedication i
Acknowledgments ii
Author Biography iii
Preface v
Chapter 1 1
Chapter 2: The Purpose Principle 7
Chapter 3: Self-Discovery 13
Chapter 4: Overcoming Barriers 18
Chapter 5: Setting Intentions 24
Chapter 6: Cultivating Mindfulness 30
Chapter 7: Building a Support Network 36
Chapter 8: Taking Action 42
Chapter 9: Living Authentically 48
Chapter 10: Sustaining Your Purpose 54

Preface

We live in a noisy world filled with constant advice, shifting expectations, and pressure to always do more and be more. But in the quiet moments, a different question sometimes surfaces: *Is this really the life I want to live?*

Living with Intention is an answer to that question.

Not the final answer, but a beginning. A way. A series of soft steps that take you back to clarity, self-understanding, and direction. Through true stories, psychological insights, and practical tools, this book invites you to take a moment to listen to your life, not the one you show the world, but the one that exists beneath it.

You won't find magic fixes here. But you will find permission to question, to rediscover, and to choose with intention. You'll discover how to tune into your values, dig up your passions, and confront the fears and expectations that hold you back.

You'll also be introduced to people, not perfect people, but authentic ones, who decided to listen to that little voice within, and what came next when they did.

Regardless of whether you're at a breaking point, a turning point, or simply wondering what comes next, this book was written with one hope: to remind you that your life can still be influenced by what is most important to you.

Chapter 1

The Concept of Intention

Intention is not merely a fleeting thought; it is a powerful, driving force that can shape our lives in profound ways. When we set an intention, we are essentially declaring our desires and goals to the universe. This declaration is not just about what we want to achieve; it reflects our deepest values and aspirations. For instance, a young woman named Clara set an intention to help others after witnessing the struggles of her community during a crisis. By focusing her energy on this intention, she found her calling in social work, transforming her life and the lives of countless others.

Scientific research shows that having clear intentions can significantly affect our behaviour and outcomes. Studies in psychology suggest that when we articulate our intentions, we activate neural pathways that align our actions with our goals. It's akin to programming a GPS for a journey; without a clear destination, we may wander aimlessly. One compelling example is the story of a group of athletes who visualised their goals before competitions. Their focused intentions resulted in improved performances, illustrating the tangible power of intention in achieving success.

To live with intention, one must begin by identifying personal values and passions. This process can be enlightening, often prompting introspection about what truly matters in life. For example, a middle-aged man named Tom spent years in a corporate job that left him unfulfilled. After taking time to reflect on his passions, he realised he wanted to pursue art. By setting an intention to explore this passion, he took the leap to become a full-time artist, discovering joy and purpose in his life.

Once intentions are set, the next step is to take actionable steps towards achieving them. This might involve creating a vision board, setting specific goals, or even seeking mentorship from those who have walked a similar path. Sarah, a recent college graduate, utilised these techniques by attending workshops and connecting with professionals in her desired field. Her commitment to her intention not only opened doors but also built her confidence, proving that intention coupled with action can lead to remarkable transformations.

Ultimately, embracing the concept of intention is about taking responsibility for our lives and choices. It invites us to consider what we truly want and empowers us to pursue it with passion and determination. As we navigate our journeys, let us remember the stories of individuals like Clara, Tom, and Sarah, who have followed their intentions to create meaningful lives. By living intentionally, we can all discover our purpose and contribute positively to the world around us.

The Importance of Living with Purpose

Living with purpose is not merely a lofty ideal; it is essential for leading a fulfilling life. When individuals engage in activities that resonate with their core values and aspirations, they experience a profound sense of satisfaction. Take the story of Sarah, a corporate lawyer who felt unfulfilled despite her success. After volunteering at a local shelter, she discovered her passion for helping others, which transformed her life. This awakening led her to shift her career towards nonprofit work, illustrating how purpose can redefine one's trajectory.

Scientific studies support the notion that living with purpose can significantly impact mental health and overall well-being. Research indicates that individuals who perceive their lives as purposeful report lower levels of anxiety and depression. For example, a study conducted by psychologists at the University of Michigan found that people with a strong sense of purpose had better cognitive function as they aged. This evidence underscores the importance of aligning one's daily actions with a greater mission.

To find your purpose, it is crucial to engage in self-reflection and exploration. Consider what activities bring you joy and fulfilment. Start by listing moments in your life where you felt truly alive and connected. For instance, John, a teacher, realised his purpose lay in inspiring young minds after reflecting on the impact of his favourite mentors. By taking small, intentional steps towards your passions, you can gradually uncover your unique calling.

Another key aspect of living with purpose is setting clear goals that align with your values. Goals serve as a roadmap, guiding you towards your desired destination. Emily, an aspiring artist, began creating a vision board to visualise her dreams. This tangible representation of her aspirations kept her motivated, even during challenging times. By breaking down her larger goals into manageable tasks, she was able to make steady progress towards a fulfilling career in the arts.

Ultimately, living with purpose is about more than personal fulfilment; it also has the potential to create a positive ripple effect in the world. When individuals pursue their passions, they inspire others to do the same. A community of purpose-driven individuals can foster collaboration and innovation, leading to transformative change. As you embark on your journey to discover your purpose, remember that your unique contributions can make a significant difference in the lives of those around you.

Stories of Transformation

Stories of transformation are powerful narratives that resonate with us all. They remind us that change is possible, no matter how insurmountable our challenges may seem. Take the story of Sarah, a woman who spent years feeling unfulfilled in her corporate job. One day, a chance encounter with a mentor ignited her passion for environmental conservation. With courage and determination, she left her stable job to pursue a career dedicated to saving the planet. Her journey illustrates that our true calling often lies just beyond our comfort zone, waiting for us to take that first step.

In science, we find evidence supporting the idea that transformation is integral to the human experience. Research shows that individuals who align their lives with their passions report higher levels of happiness and satisfaction. This is exemplified in the story of Mark, who transitioned from a mundane office role to becoming a successful chef. He discovered that by following his heart and embracing his culinary skills, he not only found joy in his work but also inspired others to pursue their dreams. Such transformations are not simply personal victories; they contribute positively to society as a whole.

To embark on your own transformation, it is essential to reflect on what truly moves you. Begin by asking yourself meaningful questions: What activities make you lose track of time? What issues ignite your passion? These reflections can guide you toward uncovering your purpose. As you identify these passions, consider the story of Emma, who spent years volunteering at a local shelter. Her experience revealed her calling to work with underprivileged children, leading her to start a non-profit organisation. This step-by-step journey illustrates the importance of taking action based on your discoveries.

Transformation often requires perseverance and resilience. The story of James, who faced numerous setbacks while pursuing his dream of becoming a writer, exemplifies this perfectly. Despite countless rejections, he continued to hone his craft, ultimately publishing a bestselling novel that resonated with readers worldwide. His journey teaches us that setbacks are not roadblocks but rather stepping stones on the path to success. Embracing the challenges of transformation is crucial to achieving our true potential.

Ultimately, the stories of transformation remind us that we all possess the ability to change our lives for the better. Whether through small daily actions or significant life changes, each step we take towards our purpose leads us closer to a fulfilling life. By sharing these stories, we inspire others to embark on their journeys of self-discovery and transformation. Remember that every great achievement begins with a single step towards embracing your true self.

Chapter 2: The Purpose Principle

Defining Your Purpose

Finding your purpose is a journey that many embark on, yet few complete. It begins with introspection and asking yourself the fundamental question: what truly matters to me? This inquiry can lead you down paths of joy, fulfilment, and even hardship. For instance, consider the story of Maya, who spent years in a corporate job that drained her spirit. After much soul-searching, she discovered her passion for teaching and now inspires young minds every day. Her transformation illustrates how understanding one's purpose can lead to profound changes in life.

Science has shown that having a clear sense of purpose can significantly enhance overall well-being. Research indicates that individuals with a defined purpose experience lower levels of stress and greater resilience in the face of adversity. For example, a study published in the Journal of Happiness Studies found that those with a strong sense of purpose reported higher life satisfaction and lower rates of depression. This evidence underscores the importance of defining your purpose and how it serves as a foundation for a healthy and rewarding life.

To embark on this quest, consider taking deliberate steps to uncover your purpose. Start by reflecting on your core values and what activities bring you joy. Journaling can be a powerful tool in this process. Write about moments when you felt most alive and fulfilled. Through this practice, you may identify recurring themes that point towards your true calling. Remember, it is not only about what you love but also how you can contribute to the world with your unique gifts and experiences.

Engaging with others can also provide clarity. Share your thoughts with friends or mentors who can offer insights and encouragement. Participate in workshops or community groups that resonate with your interests. The experiences and stories of others can illuminate your path, revealing possibilities you may not have considered. Just as a compass guides a traveller, the connections you make can steer you toward your purpose.

Ultimately, defining your purpose is not a destination but an ongoing journey. It evolves as you grow and change. Embrace the process and allow yourself the grace to discover new passions and aspirations along the way. Just like the ocean tides, your purpose may ebb and flow, but each phase brings with it lessons and opportunities for growth. By committing to this journey, you not only enrich your own life but also inspire those around you to seek their own paths of fulfilment.

The Science Behind Purposeful Living

Living with purpose is not just a lofty ideal; it is rooted in science and can profoundly impact our well-being. Research shows that individuals who identify a sense of purpose experience lower levels of stress and anxiety, leading to improved mental health. For instance, a study conducted by psychologists revealed that those who reported a strong sense of purpose in life were 15% more likely to live longer than their counterparts. This connection between purpose and longevity illustrates how foundational a sense of direction can be in our lives.

Stories abound of individuals who have transformed their lives by discovering their purpose. Consider the tale of a man who, after a successful career in finance, felt unfulfilled. He took a leap of faith and started a non-profit organisation that supports underprivileged children. Through this journey, he not only found joy but also an overwhelming sense of accomplishment. His story exemplifies how embracing one's purpose can lead to personal fulfilment and inspire others along the way.

The science behind purposeful living is also linked to the release of neurotransmitters such as dopamine and oxytocin, which are associated with feelings of happiness and connection. Engaging in activities that resonate with our core values boosts these chemicals, enhancing our overall sense of well-being. This biological response highlights the importance of aligning our daily actions with our purpose, as it fosters both emotional and physical health.

To embark on your journey towards discovering your purpose, start by reflecting on your passions and values. Consider journaling your thoughts, as this process can help illuminate what truly matters to you. Additionally, seek experiences that challenge and excite you; these can act as catalysts for self-discovery. Surrounding yourself with like-minded individuals who share your aspirations can also provide support and motivation along the way.

Ultimately, living with intention requires continuous exploration and commitment. It is a dynamic process, often involving trial and error. Embrace the journey, as each step brings you closer to a more meaningful life. By understanding the science behind purposeful living, you can unlock the potential within yourself to live fully and authentically, making a positive impact on the world around you.

Recognising Your Unique Gifts

Recognising your unique gifts is a vital step in the journey to living with intention and purpose. Each of us possesses inherent talents and strengths that, when identified, can guide us towards fulfilling our true calling. Consider the story of a young woman named Emma, who discovered her passion for art after years of working in a corporate job. It was only when she participated in a community art project that she realised how much joy creating brought her. This moment of clarity set her on a path to pursue art full-time, illustrating how recognising our gifts can change our lives for the better.

Scientific research supports the idea that understanding our unique abilities can significantly impact our overall well-being. Studies have shown that individuals who engage in activities aligned with their strengths experience higher levels of happiness and satisfaction. For instance, a study published in the Journal of Happiness Studies found that people who use their skills and talents regularly reported a greater sense of purpose. This evidence highlights the importance of not only recognising our gifts but also embracing them in our daily lives, as they can lead us to a more fulfilled existence.

To start recognising your unique gifts, consider reflecting on your past experiences. What activities make you lose track of time? What praise do you receive from friends and colleagues? Take time to journal these insights, as they can serve as clues to your inherent talents. Additionally, seeking feedback from others can provide valuable perspectives on your strengths that you might overlook. This process of introspection and external input can help illuminate the path towards understanding your true gifts.

Another effective step is to experiment with new activities that interest you. Join workshops, volunteer, or take classes in areas you've always wanted to explore. For instance, someone who has always enjoyed cooking might discover a knack for teaching others how to cook, thus revealing a hidden talent. By stepping out of your comfort zone, you create opportunities to uncover unique gifts you never knew existed. Embracing this exploration can lead to surprising revelations about your capabilities.

Finally, remember that recognising your unique gifts is an ongoing process. It requires patience and a willingness to adapt as you grow. As you start to align your life with these gifts, you may find new passions emerging. Much like

Emma, who now runs art workshops for children, your journey can inspire others as well. By embracing your unique gifts, you not only enrich your own life but also contribute positively to the world around you.

Chapter 3: Self-Discovery

Reflecting on Your Values

Reflecting on your values is a profound journey that can unlock the door to your true purpose. Each of us carries a unique set of beliefs and principles that guide our decisions and shape our identity. Consider the story of Maya, a young woman who felt lost in her corporate job. After a weekend retreat focused on self-reflection, she realised that her passion lay in environmental conservation, leading her to a fulfilling career where she could make a difference. This illustrates how understanding your values can steer you towards a life that resonates with your authentic self.

Science supports the idea that aligning your life with your core values leads to greater satisfaction and well-being. Research has shown that individuals who engage in value-based living experience lower stress levels and higher overall happiness. For instance, a study conducted at a prominent university found that participants who reflected on their values before making decisions reported feeling more fulfilled and motivated. This evidence underscores the importance of taking the time to reflect on what truly matters to you.

To begin your own reflection, start by identifying your core values. Write down a list of what you believe is most important in life, such as integrity, love, or creativity. This process can be enlightening and may reveal aspects of yourself that you hadn't fully acknowledged. Once you have your list, prioritise these values to understand which ones resonate most deeply with you. This prioritisation can serve as a compass, guiding your choices and actions in the direction of your true calling.

Next, contemplate how these values manifest in your daily life. Are your actions aligned with your beliefs, or do you find yourself compromising? For instance, if one of your core values is family but your job consumes most of your time, you may feel a sense of conflict. Reflecting on these discrepancies can help you make necessary adjustments, ensuring that your life reflects your true priorities and aspirations.

Finally, embrace the journey of living in alignment with your values. It may require courage and perseverance, but the rewards are immeasurable. As you start to make choices that resonate with your values, you will likely notice a shift in your outlook on life. Remember Maya? Her decision to pursue her passion not only transformed her career but also enriched her life in countless ways. By reflecting on your values and living with intention, you too can unlock the extraordinary potential within you.

Identifying Your Passions

Identifying your passions is a journey of self-discovery that can lead to a more fulfilling life. Many people wander through life without truly understanding what ignites their spirit. Research shows that those who are aware of their passions tend to lead happier, more productive lives. It's important to take the time to explore your interests and values, as this exploration can guide you toward your purpose.

Stories of individuals who have embraced their passions can be incredibly inspiring. Consider the tale of a teacher who left a corporate job to start a non-profit aimed at helping underprivileged children. Her passion for education and community service transformed her life and the lives of countless others. When you hear stories like hers, it becomes clear that following your passion can lead to profound changes, not just for yourself, but for those around you.

Science supports the idea that engaging with your passions can enhance well-being. Studies have shown that people who pursue activities they love experience lower levels of stress and higher levels of satisfaction. By identifying what you truly love, you open up pathways to joy and creativity. This can be as simple as reflecting on what makes you feel alive or asking yourself when you last lost track of time because you were so engrossed in an activity.

To identify your passions, start by taking small steps. Begin with a self-assessment: list activities that bring you joy, moments when you felt most fulfilled, and subjects you could talk about for hours. Seek feedback from friends and family who know you well; they may see passions in you that you have overlooked. Keep an open mind and be willing to explore new interests, as sometimes passions can emerge from the most unexpected places.

Ultimately, the journey to identifying your passions is both personal and transformative. It requires patience and reflection, but the rewards are well worth the effort. By understanding what truly resonates with you, you can align your life with your values and aspirations, leading to a more intentional and purpose-driven existence. Embrace the process, and allow your passions to guide you toward a fulfilling life that resonates with your true self.

Tools for Self-Assessment

Self-assessment is an essential tool for anyone seeking to discover their true purpose. It involves reflecting on one's values, strengths, and passions, which can illuminate the path towards a more fulfilling life. One powerful method of self-assessment is journaling, where individuals can write freely about their thoughts and feelings. This practice not only aids in clarifying thoughts but also helps in identifying patterns in one's behaviour and desires, ultimately leading to greater self-awareness.

Another effective tool is the use of personality assessments, such as the Myers-Briggs Type Indicator or the Enneagram. These assessments can provide valuable insights into one's natural inclinations and preferences. For instance, a young woman named Sarah discovered through an Enneagram test that her tendency to avoid conflict stemmed from her desire for harmony. This realisation allowed her to confront issues more directly, leading to healthier relationships and an improved sense of purpose.

Mindfulness practices, including meditation and deep-breathing exercises, also play a crucial role in self-assessment. By quieting the mind, individuals can better listen to their inner thoughts and feelings. Take the story of John, who, after years in a corporate job, began meditating regularly. This practice helped him uncover his passion for art, which he had neglected for years. Such moments of clarity can guide individuals toward their calling and prompt them to take actionable steps in that direction.

Setting specific goals based on the insights gained from self-assessment tools is vital. Once individuals have a clearer understanding of their strengths and passions, they can create realistic and measurable goals. For example, Maria, who realised her love for helping others, set a goal to volunteer at a local shelter once a week. This commitment not only enriched her life but also brought her closer to her purpose of serving the community.

In conclusion, the journey of self-assessment is about more than just introspection; it is about taking actionable steps toward living with intention. Tools like journaling, personality assessments, mindfulness practices, and goal setting can transform one's understanding of self and pave the way toward discovering a fulfilling life purpose. By engaging with these tools, anyone can begin their journey toward a more meaningful existence, filled with passion and clarity.

Chapter 4: Overcoming Barriers

Fear and Doubt

Fear and doubt are universal experiences that can hinder our journey towards finding purpose. Many people, including successful figures like J.K. Rowling, faced immense fear and self-doubt before achieving their dreams. Rowling's story of rejection and perseverance mirrors that of many who grapple with the internal voices that tell them they are not enough. Recognising these feelings is the first step in overcoming them, as it allows us to confront the barriers that keep us from living fully.

Science supports the notion that fear and doubt are deeply rooted in our brain's wiring. The amygdala, responsible for processing emotions, can trigger a fight-or-flight response when we face uncertainty. This biological reaction can lead to paralysis in decision-making and a reluctance to pursue our passions. Understanding that this reaction is a natural part of being human can help us to mitigate its effects. We can reframe our thoughts, acknowledging fear as a signal for growth rather than a stop sign.

To combat fear and doubt, it is essential to take actionable steps. Start by journaling your fears; writing them down can reduce their power over you. Additionally, setting small, achievable goals can build confidence over time. Each small victory creates a ripple effect, enabling you to tackle larger challenges. This method has been effective for many, including entrepreneurs who started with a single idea and built their empires step by step.

Community support is another powerful tool in overcoming fear and doubt. Sharing your experiences with others facing similar challenges can create a safe space for growth. Whether through support groups, workshops, or online forums, connecting with like-minded individuals can inspire you to keep pushing forward. Many have found that their purpose becomes clearer when they collaborate and share their journeys with others, reinforcing the idea that we are not alone in our struggles.

Ultimately, living with intention means acknowledging fear and doubt but not allowing them to dictate our lives. Embracing vulnerability can lead to profound personal growth and the discovery of your true calling. Remember, even the most accomplished individuals have faced their own fears and doubts. By taking conscious steps to confront these feelings, you can move closer to living a life filled with purpose and passion.

Societal Expectations

In today's world, societal expectations exert an enormous influence on our lives. From a young age, we are conditioned to conform to certain norms and standards set by our families, peers, and communities. For instance, the pressure to pursue specific careers, marry at a certain age, or achieve particular milestones can be overwhelming. These expectations can lead individuals to follow paths that may not resonate with their true selves, often causing a deep sense of dissatisfaction and unfulfillment. Understanding how these societal pressures shape our choices is the first step toward reclaiming our purpose.

Research in psychology highlights the impact of societal expectations on mental health. Studies show that individuals who feel compelled to meet these external standards often experience anxiety and stress. Take the story of Sarah, a talented artist who felt she had to abandon her passion for painting to pursue a more conventional job in finance. Despite her success in that field, she felt a constant void in her life, ultimately leading to burnout. Sarah's journey underscores the importance of recognising the difference between societal expectations and personal fulfilment, prompting us to question whether the paths we choose truly align with our inner desires.

To navigate societal expectations effectively, we must first engage in self-reflection. This involves asking ourselves what we genuinely want versus what we believe we should want. A practical step is to create a vision board that encapsulates your dreams and aspirations, free from external pressures. This visual representation can serve as a daily reminder to stay true to yourself. Additionally, speaking with like-minded individuals can provide encouragement and validation as you pursue your authentic path, reinforcing that you are not alone in your journey.

Another vital aspect is the courage to challenge societal norms. It can be daunting to go against the grain, but stories of individuals who have done so can inspire us. For example, consider the entrepreneur who left a lucrative corporate job to start a non-profit focused on environmental conservation. Their journey was not without struggle, but their commitment to their purpose brought immense satisfaction and impact, proving that living with intention often requires us to defy conventional expectations.

Ultimately, living intentionally means making choices that reflect our values and passions, rather than merely conforming to societal pressures. By understanding the weight of these expectations and actively working to align our lives with our true purpose, we can lead more fulfilling lives. It is essential to remember that our worth is not defined by external standards but by the authenticity of our journey. Embrace the challenge of carving your own path, and you may just uncover a life rich with meaning and purpose.

Building Resilience

Building resilience is essential for navigating the ups and downs of life. It is the ability to bounce back from setbacks and adapt to change, which is increasingly important in our fast-paced world. Research shows that resilient individuals often possess a strong sense of purpose, enabling them to face challenges head-on. For instance, consider the story of a woman who lost her job during a recession. Instead of succumbing to despair, she used this opportunity to explore her passions, eventually launching a successful business that aligned with her true calling.

The science behind resilience reveals that our brains are wired for adaptability. Neuroscience has shown that when we face adversity, our brains can rewire themselves, allowing us to develop new coping mechanisms. This is evident in the experiences of veterans returning from combat. Many find that their hardships foster a sense of community and purpose, which aids in their recovery. They often share their stories, emphasising how embracing their vulnerabilities led to personal growth and stronger relationships.

To build resilience, it is crucial to embrace a growth mindset. This means viewing challenges as opportunities for learning rather than insurmountable obstacles. Take the example of a student struggling with maths; by reframing their perspective and seeking help, they can achieve significant improvement. Setting small, achievable goals can also foster a sense of accomplishment and build confidence, further reinforcing resilience in the face of future challenges.

Another key aspect of resilience is the importance of social connections. Building a support network can provide encouragement and practical help when times get tough. Stories abound of individuals who have relied on friends and family during difficult periods, finding strength in their shared experiences. For example, a group of friends who faced personal losses came together to support one another, ultimately discovering their shared purpose in helping others facing similar challenges.

In conclusion, resilience is not just an innate trait; it can be cultivated through practice and intention. By understanding the science behind resilience, embracing a growth mindset, and fostering strong connections, anyone can learn to navigate life's challenges more effectively. As we pursue our purpose, let us remember that resilience is a vital tool that empowers us to live fully and authentically, even in the face of adversity.

Chapter 5: Setting Intentions

The Power of Goal Setting

Goal setting is not just a tool; it is a powerful catalyst for transformation. When we articulate our aspirations, we shift from passive wishing to active planning. Consider the story of Sarah, a young woman who dreamt of becoming a published author. By setting specific, measurable goals, she turned her vague longing into a structured path, breaking down her journey into manageable milestones. This approach not only clarified her vision but also instilled a sense of accountability that propelled her forward even on challenging days.

The science behind goal setting supports its efficacy. Research indicates that individuals who set clear goals are more likely to achieve them than those who do not. Psychologist Edwin Locke's goal-setting theory highlights that specific and challenging goals lead to higher performance. This is because goals provide direction and motivation, acting as a beacon that guides our decisions and actions. For instance, Jim, an aspiring athlete, used this principle to train for a marathon. By establishing a clear timeline and measurable benchmarks, he was able to track his progress and celebrate small victories along the way, making the journey enjoyable and rewarding.

To harness the power of goal setting, it is essential to adopt a systematic approach. Start with self-reflection to identify what truly matters to you. This can involve journaling or seeking feedback from trusted friends and mentors. Once you have a clearer understanding of your values, formulate specific goals that resonate with your purpose. For example, if personal health is a priority, set goals related to fitness and nutrition that align with your intention to live fully. These goals should inspire you and be revisited regularly to adjust as necessary.

Moreover, sharing your goals with others can amplify your commitment. When you vocalise your intentions, you create a support network that provides encouragement and accountability. Take inspiration from Martin, who shared his aspirations to start a community garden with his neighbours. Their collective enthusiasm not only motivated him but also fostered a sense of community and belonging. This social aspect of goal setting can be a game changer, transforming solitary pursuits into shared journeys towards meaningful achievements.

Ultimately, the power of goal setting lies in its ability to transform dreams into reality. It empowers individuals to take charge of their lives and pursue their passions with clarity and determination. As you embark on your own goal-setting journey, remember to celebrate every achievement, no matter how small, as each step brings you closer to living with intention. Embrace the process, and let your goals illuminate your path to finding your purpose and living fully.

Creating a Vision Board

Creating a vision board is a powerful technique that helps individuals visualise their goals and aspirations, bringing clarity to their desires. This process begins with reflection; take a moment to consider what truly matters to you. By identifying your core values and passions, you can create a focused representation of your dreams. The act of gathering images, quotes, and symbols that resonate with your intentions serves as a tangible reminder of your purpose and direction in life.

The science behind vision boards lies in the principles of visualisation and the law of attraction. Numerous studies have shown that when we visualise our goals, we activate the same neural pathways as if we are actually experiencing those achievements. This not only boosts motivation but also encourages positive habits that align with our vision. For instance, a study conducted at the Dominican University of California revealed that individuals who wrote down their goals were significantly more likely to achieve them compared to those who merely thought about them.

As you begin to create your vision board, gather materials that inspire you—magazines, photos, or even digital images from online sources. Find a quiet space where you can focus without distractions. Start by arranging your chosen images and words in a way that feels right to you. There is no right or wrong way to do this; allow your creativity to flow. Each element should resonate with your aspirations and evoke the emotions you wish to experience as you work towards your dreams.

Once your vision board is complete, display it prominently in your home or workspace. The key is to see it daily, allowing it to serve as a constant reminder of your goals. Engage with your board regularly; take time to reflect on the images and affirmations it contains. This practice not only reinforces your intentions but also helps you track your progress, making adjustments as needed. Celebrate the small victories along the way, as they are stepping stones towards your larger aspirations.

In conclusion, creating a vision board is more than just a creative exercise; it is a profound tool for self-discovery and personal growth. By committing to this practice, you align yourself with your purpose and take proactive steps towards living a fulfilling life. As you create and engage with your vision board, remember that it is a dynamic representation of your journey, one that evolves as you do, guiding you towards your true calling.

Developing an Action Plan

Developing an action plan is a crucial step in living with intention and discovering your purpose. It begins with self-reflection, where you assess your strengths, weaknesses, and passions. For instance, consider the story of Clara, who was stuck in a corporate job that didn't fulfil her. Through journaling and meditative practices, she realised her love for teaching and helping others. This awareness ignited her journey towards creating a more meaningful life, showcasing how introspection can lead to clarity in defining one's goals.

Once you have a clearer understanding of your purpose, it's time to set specific, measurable goals. This involves breaking down your larger aspirations into smaller, manageable tasks. Take the example of James, who wanted to start a community garden to promote sustainability. By setting a timeline and identifying steps such as gathering community support, securing a location, and sourcing seeds, he transformed his dream into actionable steps. This method not only makes your goals feel achievable but also provides a roadmap to guide your progress.

Accountability is a significant aspect of executing your action plan. Sharing your goals with friends or joining a support group can create a network of encouragement and motivation. For instance, Emily, who aimed to write a book, found accountability in a writers' group. Their feedback and support kept her committed to her writing schedule, illustrating the power of community in pursuing one's purpose. This shared journey fosters not only personal growth but also a sense of belonging.

As you implement your plan, be prepared to adapt and refine your approach. Life is unpredictable, and sometimes the path to your purpose may require adjustments. Consider the case of Mark, who initially aimed to open a restaurant but pivoted to a food truck due to financial constraints. This flexibility allowed him to pursue his passion in a manner that aligned with his resources, proving that resilience and adaptability are keys to overcoming obstacles on the journey to fulfilment.

Finally, celebrate your achievements, no matter how small they may seem. Acknowledging progress reinforces your motivation and commitment to your purpose. Sarah, who volunteered at a local shelter, found joy in celebrating each life she touched. By recognising her impact, she fuelled her desire to do more, demonstrating that every step taken towards your goal is a victory worth celebrating. Developing an action plan is not merely about the destination; it's about embracing the journey with intention and passion.

Chapter 6: Cultivating Mindfulness

The Role of Mindfulness in Purpose

Mindfulness serves as an essential tool in the journey towards discovering and fulfilling one's purpose. By anchoring ourselves in the present moment, we can sift through the noise of daily life and connect with our inner selves. For instance, consider Sarah, a corporate lawyer who felt unfulfilled despite her success. Through mindfulness practices such as meditation and mindful walking, she began to explore her true passions, ultimately leading her to start a non-profit organisation that aids underprivileged youth. Her journey exemplifies how mindfulness can illuminate paths that may otherwise remain obscured.

The science behind mindfulness reveals its profound effects on the brain and emotional well-being. Research shows that mindfulness can enhance focus, reduce stress, and promote emotional regulation. These benefits are crucial when seeking purpose, as they enable individuals to confront fears and uncertainties with clarity. A study published in a leading psychological journal found that participants who engaged in mindfulness meditation experienced a notable increase in life satisfaction and a deeper sense of meaning. This scientific backing reinforces the idea that mindfulness not only enriches our lives but also guides us towards our true calling.

Incorporating mindfulness into daily routines does not have to be an overwhelming task. Simple steps can be taken, such as dedicating a few minutes each day to focused breathing or practicing gratitude. For instance, John, a busy father of three, carved out ten minutes each morning to meditate. This small yet consistent practice allowed him to approach his day with a clearer mind, ultimately helping him discover a passion for coaching youth sports. His story illustrates that even the busiest individuals can find time for mindfulness, leading to significant revelations about their purpose.

Moreover, mindfulness cultivates resilience, a vital trait for anyone on the quest for purpose. Life's challenges can often feel insurmountable, but mindfulness teaches us to observe our thoughts and feelings without judgment. This perspective allows us to bounce back from setbacks and view obstacles as opportunities for growth. When Maria faced a significant career setback, she turned to mindfulness as a source of strength. Instead of succumbing to despair, she used the time to reflect on her values and eventually pivoted towards a career in holistic health, where she felt more aligned with her true self.

Ultimately, the role of mindfulness in finding purpose is about fostering a deeper connection with ourselves and the world around us. By embracing the present and nurturing our inner thoughts, we can uncover what truly matters to us. Stories like those of Sarah, John, and Maria remind us that mindfulness is not merely a practice; it is a pathway to a more intentional and fulfilling life. As we engage with our inner selves, we become equipped to live with intention, aligning our actions with our deepest values and aspirations.

Techniques for Mindful Living

Mindful living is an art that encourages us to engage fully with our lives, nurturing a deeper connection with ourselves and the world around us. One of the simplest techniques to practice mindful living is through meditation. Just as a scientist studies the intricate details of nature, we can observe our thoughts and feelings without judgement. For instance, Sarah, a busy mother, felt overwhelmed by her daily responsibilities. By dedicating just ten minutes each morning to meditation, she noticed a profound shift in her perspective, allowing her to approach challenges with clarity and calmness.

Another effective technique is the practice of gratitude. Research has shown that regularly acknowledging what we are thankful for can significantly enhance our overall well-being. Consider John, a university student who struggled with anxiety. He began a daily gratitude journal, noting down three things he appreciated each day. Over time, this simple act transformed his mindset, fostering a sense of purpose and connection to his surroundings that he had previously overlooked.

Engaging in mindful eating is yet another powerful practice. This involves savouring each bite, recognising the flavours and textures of our food, which can lead to a healthier relationship with eating. Emma, who had long battled with emotional eating, decided to turn her mealtimes into mindful experiences. By focusing solely on her meals without distractions, she discovered a newfound respect for her body and its needs, ultimately leading to healthier choices and a more fulfilling life.

Mindful walking is a technique that combines physical activity with awareness. As you walk, pay attention to the sensation of your feet touching the ground and the rhythm of your breath. This practice can be particularly grounding and rejuvenating. For example, Mark, an office worker, took short walks during his breaks, immersing himself in the sounds of nature. These moments of mindfulness not only reduced his stress but also inspired him to appreciate the beauty in everyday life.

Lastly, cultivating compassion towards oneself and others is vital in mindful living. Research supports that self-compassion can improve emotional resilience. Lisa, a teacher, started practising self-kindness during challenging days. By treating herself with the same compassion she offered her students, she found an inner strength that allowed her to connect more deeply with others. Through these various techniques, we can all learn to live with intention, embracing our purpose and finding fulfilment in the present moment.

Embracing the Present Moment

In our fast-paced world, the art of embracing the present moment is often overlooked. We find ourselves caught in a web of distractions, chasing future goals or ruminating over past mistakes. Yet, the key to unlocking a fulfilling life lies in our ability to be fully present. Mindfulness, a practice rooted in ancient traditions, has gained scientific backing, showing its profound impact on our overall well-being and purpose. Studies reveal that those who engage in mindfulness tend to experience greater emotional resilience, improved focus, and a deeper connection to their lives.

Consider the story of Sarah, a busy professional who spent years climbing the corporate ladder, only to realise she was missing out on life's simplest pleasures. One day, during her commute, she decided to put her phone away and truly observe the world around her. She noticed the vibrant colours of the trees, the laughter of children playing, and the warmth of the sun on her skin. This simple act of being present transformed her perspective and reignited her passion for life. By embracing the present moment, Sarah found clarity in her purpose, allowing her to align her career with her true values and desires.

Embracing the present moment requires intentional steps. Start by setting aside a few minutes each day for mindfulness practice. This could involve meditation, deep breathing exercises, or simply taking a walk in nature. During these moments, focus on your senses; notice the sounds, smells, and textures around you. Gradually, you will cultivate a heightened awareness that can profoundly enhance your daily experiences. Additionally, journaling about your present moments can solidify this practice, helping you reflect on your feelings and insights.

The science behind mindfulness illustrates its benefits on mental health. Research indicates that regular mindfulness practice can reduce anxiety and depression, leading to a more balanced emotional state. Neuroscientific studies show changes in brain structure associated with increased mindfulness, including improved connectivity in areas responsible for emotional regulation and self awareness. By understanding the science, we can appreciate the power of being present and its role in discovering our true purpose.

Ultimately, embracing the present moment is a journey, not a destination. It invites us to let go of our fears and expectations, allowing us to experience life authentically. As we learn to live in the now, we become more attuned to our inner selves and the world around us. This shift not only enhances our personal growth but also fosters a greater connection with others. By integrating mindfulness into our daily lives, we can unlock the door to living fully and with intention, ultimately leading us towards our unique calling.

Chapter 7: Building a Support Network

The Importance of Community

In today's interconnected world, the importance of community cannot be overstated. Research shows that individuals who engage with their communities are often happier and healthier than those who do not. Take the story of Sarah, a single mother who moved to a new city and felt isolated. By joining a local support group, she not only found friends but also discovered a renewed sense of purpose that transformed her outlook on life. This illustrates how community can act as a catalyst for personal growth and fulfilment.

Moreover, communities provide a platform for shared experiences and collective wisdom. When we come together, we share our stories, struggles, and triumphs, creating a tapestry of human connection. For instance, a small town in Italy came together to restore a dilapidated community centre. Through their collaborative effort, not only did they beautify their surroundings, but they also strengthened their bonds and created a space for future generations. This serves as a powerful reminder of how working together can enhance our sense of belonging.

The science behind community engagement reveals that social connections can enhance our mental and physical well-being. Studies indicate that individuals who are socially active have lower stress levels and a decreased risk of chronic illnesses. For example, a research project in Norway found that participants who volunteered regularly reported higher life satisfaction and lower depression rates. This underscores the idea that investing in community is, in fact, investing in ourselves and our health.

Taking steps to engage with your community can be as simple as attending local events, volunteering, or starting a conversation with a neighbour. Each small action can lead to meaningful connections. Consider the journey of John, who began by volunteering at a local charity. He not only made friends but also found his calling in helping others, ultimately leading him to start his own non-profit organisation. This highlights the transformative power that community involvement can have on our lives.

In conclusion, the importance of community is profound and multifaceted. It enriches our lives, provides support, and fosters personal growth. By actively participating in our communities, we not only enhance our own lives but also contribute to the well-being of those around us. As we seek to live with intention and discover our purpose, let us remember that our communities are vital to our journey, providing the support and connection we need to thrive.

Finding Mentors and Role Models

Finding mentors and role models is a pivotal step in the journey towards understanding your purpose. These individuals can provide guidance, support, and inspiration as you navigate the complexities of life. For instance, consider the story of J.K. Rowling, who faced numerous rejections before her Harry Potter series became a global phenomenon. It was the encouragement of her mentor that helped her persevere and ultimately achieve her dreams. Such stories highlight the importance of having someone who believes in you and your potential.

Research shows that mentorship can significantly impact personal and professional growth. A study by the American Psychological Association found that mentees are more likely to advance in their careers, have higher job satisfaction, and even earn more than those without mentors. This underscores the idea that mentorship is not just about guidance; it’s about opening doors and creating opportunities that may otherwise remain closed. By seeking out mentors who resonate with your values and aspirations, you can enhance your path towards finding your calling.

Finding the right mentor or role model requires intentionality and effort. Start by identifying individuals who inspire you, whether they are in your field or from diverse backgrounds. Attend networking events, workshops, or online forums where you can connect with potential mentors. Don't hesitate to reach out and express your admiration for their work; many are willing to share their knowledge and experiences. Remember, the key is to be genuine in your approach, as authenticity often fosters meaningful connections.

Moreover, role models are not limited to those who are famous or highly successful. Look around you; your mentor could be a teacher, a community leader, or even a family member who embodies the values you aspire to uphold. Learning from their experiences and insights can provide a unique perspective on your own journey. Embrace the idea that everyone has something to teach you, and be open to the lessons that come from unexpected sources.

In conclusion, finding mentors and role models is a crucial component of living with intention and discovering your purpose. Their insights can illuminate your path, helping you navigate challenges and celebrate successes along the way. As you embark on this quest, remember that building these relationships takes time and effort, but the rewards are immeasurable. Embrace the journey, and let the wisdom of those who have walked the path before you guide you towards a fulfilling life.

Engaging with Like-minded Individuals

Engaging with like-minded individuals is a powerful catalyst for personal growth and the discovery of one's purpose. When we surround ourselves with people who share our values and aspirations, we create an environment that nurtures our ambitions. Consider the story of a young artist who felt isolated in her pursuit of creativity. By joining a local art collective, she not only found inspiration but also forged deep connections that encouraged her to explore her talents further. This illustrates how community can elevate our journey toward living with intention.

Research supports the notion that social connections significantly impact our mental well-being and life satisfaction. A study published in the Journal of Happiness Studies found that individuals who actively engage in communities tend to report higher levels of happiness and fulfilment. This is because these relationships provide support, encouragement, and accountability. By engaging with others who share our passions, we can share our struggles and triumphs, leading to a richer, more meaningful experience in our pursuits.

Finding these like-minded individuals requires a proactive approach. Start by identifying your interests and values, then seek out groups, workshops, or online forums that resonate with you. For instance, if you are passionate about environmental sustainability, consider joining local activism groups or participating in community clean-up events. This not only allows you to contribute positively to the world but also connects you with others who share your vision and drive.

Once you find your tribe, it is essential to foster these relationships. Make time for regular meet-ups, whether in person or virtually, to share ideas and support one another's journeys. As an example, a group of aspiring writers may set weekly sessions to discuss their progress and share feedback. These gatherings can transform into a sanctuary where you feel safe to express your thoughts and dreams, reinforcing the belief that you are not alone in your quest for purpose.

In conclusion, engaging with like-minded individuals enriches our lives immeasurably. It offers us a sense of belonging and motivates us to pursue our passions with renewed vigour. Take the step today to reach out and connect with others; you may just find that the support and inspiration you seek have been waiting for you all along. Together, we can create a world where everyone feels empowered to live fully and intentionally, discovering their unique purpose along the way.

Chapter 8: Taking Action

Small Steps Towards Your Purpose

Finding your purpose can seem like a daunting task, but it often begins with small, intentional steps. Consider the story of Sarah, a young woman who felt lost in her corporate job. She decided to dedicate just fifteen minutes a day to explore her interests. This small commitment led her to discover her passion for photography, and eventually she transitioned to a career that fulfilled her heart's desire. Sarah's journey illustrates how even the smallest actions can lead to significant transformations.

Scientific research supports the idea that incremental changes can lead to substantial outcomes. Behavioural psychologists have found that setting achievable goals and taking small steps can vastly improve motivation and success rates. This principle is often referred to as the "small wins" theory, which posits that celebrating minor achievements can create a positive feedback loop, encouraging individuals to continue pursuing their larger goals. By applying this concept to our quest for purpose, we can make the process less overwhelming and more manageable.

To start your journey, reflect on what truly brings you joy. Take a moment each day to write down one thing that made you smile or sparked your interest. Over time, patterns will emerge, illuminating the paths that resonate with your essence. For example, if you find joy in volunteering, consider dedicating a few hours each week to a local charity. These small acts of service not only connect you with your community but also help you discover your calling in the process.

Another effective strategy is to seek inspiration from others. Join workshops, attend talks, or engage in online communities where you can learn from those who have walked a similar path. Hearing stories of resilience and discovery can ignite a spark within you, motivating you to take your own small steps. Remember, everyone's journey is unique, and learning from others can provide invaluable insights and encouragement.

Finally, be patient with yourself. The journey to finding your purpose is not a race; it is a personal exploration that unfolds over time. Celebrate each small step you take, knowing that they are all vital components of your greater journey. Embrace the process, and trust that with each step, you are moving closer to living a life filled with intention and purpose.

Embracing Change and Adaptability

Embracing change is an essential part of living with intention and finding your purpose. Change is a constant in life, and those who accept it are often the ones who thrive. When we resist change, we can find ourselves stuck in routines that no longer serve us. Instead, by welcoming change, we open ourselves to new experiences, perspectives, and opportunities that can lead us closer to our true calling.

The story of a young woman who left her stable job to pursue her passion for art illustrates this beautifully. She found that stepping out of her comfort zone allowed her to discover talents she never knew she had.

Adaptability goes hand in hand with embracing change. In a world that is continuously evolving, those who can adjust their sails will weather the storms of uncertainty. Science supports this notion, revealing that adaptable individuals often possess a growth mindset, which allows them to see challenges as opportunities for learning and development. Consider the remarkable story of a community that faced severe flooding. Instead of succumbing to despair, the residents banded together to create a new plan for their town, demonstrating how adaptability can lead to resilience and regeneration.

To cultivate a mindset of adaptability, one must first recognise the importance of self-awareness. Understanding your strengths and weaknesses can help you navigate change more effectively. Journaling can be a powerful tool in this regard, as it allows you to reflect on your experiences and emotions. Additionally, seeking feedback from others can provide valuable insights into how you can adapt to new situations. The journey of a woman who transformed her career through self-reflection and openness to feedback is a testament to the power of this step.

Another critical aspect of embracing change is fostering a supportive network. Surrounding yourself with individuals who encourage growth and exploration can significantly enhance your ability to adapt. A mentor or a supportive friend can provide guidance during times of uncertainty. The story of a young entrepreneur who sought advice from experienced business owners highlights how community support can inspire confidence and provide practical strategies for navigating change.

Ultimately, embracing change and adaptability is a lifelong practice that enriches our lives and aligns us with our purpose. Every step taken towards accepting change is a step towards personal growth. By sharing stories of resilience, leveraging science-backed strategies, and taking actionable steps, we can inspire ourselves and others to live intentionally. The journey may be challenging, but the rewards of discovering and living your purpose are immeasurable.

Celebrating Progress

In our journey towards finding purpose, celebrating progress plays a vital role. Each small victory, no matter how insignificant it may seem, contributes to our overall growth. Consider the story of a young woman named Maria, who spent years feeling lost until she began to track her daily achievements. By acknowledging her progress, she transformed her mindset and became more motivated to pursue her dreams. This teaches us that recognising even the smallest steps forward can lead to significant changes in our lives.

Scientific research supports the idea that celebrating progress enhances our motivation and well-being. Studies have shown that individuals who take time to acknowledge their accomplishments experience lower levels of stress and higher levels of satisfaction. This psychological principle is rooted in the concept of positive reinforcement, which suggests that rewarding ourselves for our efforts encourages continued progress. As we reflect on our achievements, we create a positive feedback loop that fuels our desire to push further.

To effectively celebrate progress, it's essential to set clear, achievable goals. Break down larger objectives into smaller milestones that can be recognised along the way. For instance, if your goal is to start a new career, celebrate completing each stage, such as updating your CV or attending networking events. This structured approach allows you to appreciate the journey while keeping your ultimate purpose in sight. Remember, every step taken is a step closer to realising your calling.

Another powerful way to celebrate progress is through sharing our journeys with others. When we vocalise our achievements, we invite support and encouragement from our community. Consider the story of James, who shared his progress on a social media platform. The positive responses he received not only motivated him to continue but also inspired others to pursue their paths. This collective celebration fosters a sense of belonging and accountability, which can be incredibly empowering.

Finally, make it a habit to reflect regularly on your progress. Set aside time each month to journal about your achievements, no matter how small. This practice not only reinforces your journey but also allows you to assess what strategies are working. By celebrating progress in this way, you cultivate a deeper connection with your purpose and remain committed to living intentionally. Embrace every achievement, for they are the building blocks of a fulfilling life.

Chapter 9: Living Authentically

Aligning Actions with Values

Aligning your actions with your values is a fundamental step in living a purposeful life. When your daily decisions resonate with what truly matters to you, it creates a sense of harmony and fulfilment. For instance, consider the story of a corporate executive who felt unfulfilled despite his success. After reflecting on his core values, he realised that he prioritised family and community over profit. By altering his career path to focus on a non-profit organisation, he found a deeper sense of satisfaction and joy in his work, demonstrating how aligning actions with values can profoundly impact one's life.

Science supports the notion that alignment between values and actions leads to greater well-being. Research in psychology shows that when people act in accordance with their personal values, they experience lower levels of stress and higher levels of happiness. For example, individuals who engage in volunteer work often report increased life satisfaction because their actions reflect their values of compassion and community service. This evidence suggests that aligning actions with values is not just a philosophical idea but a practical pathway to enhancing one's quality of life.

To begin aligning your actions with your values, start by identifying what truly matters to you. Take time for introspection; write down your core values and reflect on experiences that brought you joy or fulfilment. This exercise can reveal patterns and priorities that you may not have consciously acknowledged. Once you have a clear understanding of your values, assess your current actions and determine if they reflect those values. This step is crucial, as it highlights areas of your life that may require adjustment to achieve greater alignment.

Next, set tangible goals that embody your values. For instance, if one of your core values is health, consider setting a goal to exercise regularly or prepare nutritious meals. These goals act as actionable steps towards integrating your values into your daily life. Moreover, share your goals with friends or family members to create accountability. This social support can reinforce your commitment and encourage you to stay aligned with your values, even when faced with challenges.

Finally, regularly reflect on your progress and make adjustments as needed. Life is dynamic, and your values may evolve over time. By periodically assessing your actions and their alignment with your values, you ensure that you are living authentically. Embracing this ongoing process of alignment can empower you to live with intention and purpose, ultimately leading to a more fulfilling life. In doing so, you not only enrich your own existence but also inspire those around you to seek their own alignment, creating a ripple effect of positive change in the world.

The Impact of Authentic Living

Authentic living is transformative, shaping not only our individual experiences but also the world around us. When we live authentically, we align our actions with our true selves, fostering a sense of fulfilment. For instance, consider the story of Sarah, a corporate lawyer who left her high-paying job to start a non-profit aimed at helping underprivileged children. This leap, though daunting, led her to a life brimming with joy and purpose, illustrating how authenticity can lead to profound changes in one's life and the lives of others.

Scientific studies support the benefits of authentic living, indicating that individuals who embrace their true selves experience higher levels of happiness and lower levels of stress. Research from the University of California shows that authenticity is linked to greater life satisfaction. When we are true to ourselves, we create a ripple effect, inspiring others to also pursue their authentic paths. This interconnectedness highlights a crucial aspect of living with intention; our choices can significantly impact our communities, encouraging a culture of authenticity.

To embark on a journey of authentic living, it is essential to take deliberate steps towards self-discovery. Begin by reflecting on your values and passions. Journaling can be a powerful tool in this process. For example, writing down moments when you felt truly happy can help identify what brings you joy. Once you understand your core values, align your daily actions with them. This alignment not only fuels your personal growth but also inspires those around you to seek their own authenticity.

Moreover, authentic living often involves overcoming societal expectations and pressures. Many people feel compelled to conform to norms that do not resonate with their true selves. Take the example of James, who pursued a career in finance because it was deemed prestigious, yet he longed to be an artist. By breaking free from these constraints, he found not only his passion but also a supportive community that celebrated his authentic self. This narrative reinforces the importance of courage in the pursuit of a life lived with intention.

Ultimately, the impact of authentic living extends well beyond individual gratification; it contributes to a more compassionate and understanding society. As more individuals embrace their true identities, we cultivate a world that values diversity and personal expression. By sharing our stories and supporting one another, we create a collective movement that champions authenticity, urging everyone to live fully and with intention.

Stories of Authenticity

In a world often overshadowed by superficiality, stories of authenticity shine like beacons of hope. Consider the story of Sarah, a woman who left her corporate job to pursue her passion for pottery. Initially met with skepticism, she found joy and a sense of purpose in crafting unique pieces that resonated with her true self. Her journey illustrates how embracing authenticity can lead to fulfilment, drawing others to her genuine spirit and creating a community around shared values.

Research supports the notion that living authentically is linked to greater life satisfaction. A study conducted by psychologists at the University of California found that individuals who aligned their actions with their true selves reported higher levels of happiness and lower stress. This scientific backing reinforces the importance of authenticity in our lives, encouraging us to reflect on who we truly are and what we desire.

To embark on your journey towards authenticity, start by identifying your core values. Reflect on moments in your life when you felt truly alive—what were you doing, and who were you with? These experiences can offer insight into your passions and purpose. Write down these values and consider how they can guide your decisions moving forward.

Another significant step is the practice of vulnerability. Sharing your authentic self with others can be daunting, yet it fosters deeper connections. For example, John, a community leader, shared his struggles with mental health at a local event. His honesty not only helped him heal but also inspired others to open up about their own challenges, creating a supportive environment where authenticity thrives.

Ultimately, stories of authenticity remind us that the journey to discovering our purpose is deeply personal and often intertwined with the stories of others. By embracing our true selves and sharing our journeys, we not only enrich our lives but also inspire those around us to embark on their own paths to authenticity. This ripple effect can transform communities, proving that when we live with intention, we pave the way for others to do the same.

Chapter 10: Sustaining Your Purpose

Continual Growth and Learning

Continual growth and learning are essential components of living with intention and discovering your true purpose. Each day presents us with opportunities to learn and expand our horizons, both personally and professionally. For instance, consider the story of a young woman who, after years of working in a corporate job, decided to take evening classes in pottery. This small shift not only ignited her passion for creativity but also opened doors to a community that valued her unique talents, ultimately leading her to a fulfilling career as an artist.

The science behind continual growth illustrates that our brains are remarkably adaptable; this phenomenon is known as neuroplasticity. Research indicates that engaging in new experiences and challenges can enhance our cognitive abilities and emotional resilience. By embracing a mindset of lifelong learning, we can improve our capacity to handle life's uncertainties and enhance our overall well-being. Imagine a man in his fifties who, after losing his job, took the plunge into learning digital marketing, transforming his career and life trajectory in the process.

To cultivate a culture of continual growth, we must take deliberate steps toward learning. Setting aside time for self-improvement, whether through reading, online courses, or workshops, can significantly impact our development. For instance, a group of friends formed a book club, committing to read and discuss a new book each month. This simple act not only deepened their friendships but also broadened their perspectives, illustrating how shared learning can foster growth.

Moreover, it is important to reflect on our experiences to extract valuable lessons. Keeping a journal to record insights and progress can help us recognise patterns and areas for improvement. A woman who started journaling her daily reflections discovered that her struggles with procrastination stemmed from a fear of failure. By identifying this, she was able to take actionable steps to confront her fears, leading to greater productivity and satisfaction.

In conclusion, continual growth and learning are not just personal endeavours; they are vital for finding and living your purpose. As we venture through life, let us embrace every opportunity to learn, adapt, and evolve. The stories of those who have embraced this journey remind us that it is never too late to pursue our passions and redefine our goals. By fostering a commitment to learning, we can create a fulfilling life that resonates with our true calling.

Revisiting and Refining Your Purpose

Revisiting and refining your purpose is an essential journey that invites you to reflect on your life and aspirations. Many individuals find themselves at a crossroads, questioning whether their current path aligns with their true calling. Take, for instance, the story of Sarah, who after years in a corporate job, realised that her passion lay in teaching. By revisiting her purpose, she discovered a deeper fulfilment that transformed her life dramatically. This process often involves a blend of introspection, evaluation, and embracing change.

Scientific research supports the idea that having a clear sense of purpose significantly enhances our well-being. A study conducted by psychologists found that individuals with a defined purpose tend to experience lower levels of stress and greater life satisfaction. This reinforces the idea that revisiting what truly matters to us can lead to healthier, more fulfilled lives. As you reflect on your own purpose, consider the activities that energise you and the values that resonate deeply within.

To effectively refine your purpose, begin by asking yourself a series of probing questions. What activities make you lose track of time? What issues stir a sense of urgency within you? By identifying these elements, you can create a clearer picture of what your purpose might entail. For example, Mark, an environmental activist, was drawn to nature from a young age. By recognising this passion, he was able to channel his energy into meaningful work that not only fulfilled him but also made a positive impact on the planet.

Incorporating feedback from trusted friends and mentors can also provide invaluable insights. They may see strengths and passions in you that you might overlook. Engaging in open conversations about your aspirations can illuminate blind spots and inspire new directions. When Emily shared her desire to write, her friend encouraged her to pursue a blog, leading her to connect with an audience that valued her voice and perspective. Such connections can be pivotal in refining your purpose.

Lastly, remember that refining your purpose is an ongoing process. Life circumstances change, and so do we. Embrace the idea that your purpose can evolve as you gain new experiences and insights. Regularly revisiting your purpose not only keeps you aligned with your true self but also enhances your resilience in the face of challenges. Just as the seasons change, so too can your purpose, allowing you to live fully and authentically in every chapter of your life.

Leaving a Legacy

Leaving a legacy is about more than just what we leave behind; it's about how we live our lives today. Each moment presents us with an opportunity to impact others positively and contribute to something greater than ourselves. Consider the story of a schoolteacher who dedicated her life to educating underprivileged children. Years later, her former students became successful individuals who credit her guidance as the catalyst for their achievements. This demonstrates that the essence of leaving a legacy lies in nurturing potential and fostering growth in others.

Science supports the idea that meaningful connections and contributions enhance our sense of purpose. Research has shown that individuals who engage in altruistic behaviour often report higher levels of happiness and fulfilment. This is not merely anecdotal; studies indicate that helping others activates areas of the brain associated with pleasure and reward. Therefore, when we focus on leaving a legacy, we are not only enriching the lives of others but also enhancing our own well-being.

To leave a lasting legacy, we must start by identifying our core values and passions. This involves introspection and a deep understanding of what truly matters to us. Engaging in activities aligned with our values allows us to make meaningful contributions. For instance, if you value environmental sustainability, consider volunteering for local conservation projects or advocating for policy changes. Each small action, driven by your purpose, contributes to a more significant legacy.

As we take steps towards leaving our legacy, storytelling becomes a powerful tool. Sharing our experiences and the lessons we've learned can inspire others to embark on their journeys. A retired firefighter, for example, shares his stories of bravery and camaraderie, encouraging young people to pursue careers in public service. By articulating our journeys, we not only honour our past but also empower others to create their own paths, thereby extending our legacy.

Ultimately, leaving a legacy is a conscious choice that requires us to live intentionally. It involves making decisions that reflect our values and aspirations, creating ripples of positive change in the lives of those around us. As we strive to live with intention, we must remember that the legacies we leave are often formed through the relationships we build and the impacts we make along the way. By embracing this challenge, we can ensure that our lives resonate long after we are gone. It's a beautiful day.

www.ingramcontent.com/pod-product-compliance
Lightning Source LLC
LaVergne TN
LVHW022320200926
848481LV00004B/1380
* 9 7 9 8 8 9 9 7 9 7 7 9 8 *